Life Lines Flowing Through Time

Poems by Vivian Carole Gass

VIVIAN CAROLE GASS

WestBow
PRESS®
A DIVISION OF THOMAS NELSON
& ZONDERVAN

WestBow Press books may be ordered through booksellers or by contacting:

WestBow Press
A Division of Thomas Nelson & Zondervan
1663 Liberty Drive
Bloomington, IN 47403
www.westbowpress.com
844-714-3454

ISBN: 978-1-6642-5493-0 (sc)
ISBN: 978-1-6642-5492-3 (e)

Print information available on the last page.

WestBow Press rev. date: 02/11/2022

CONTENTS

DEDICATION

I dedicate this book to my beloved daughters, Rachel Grace Wolfram and Jane Allison Gavril, and to the memory of my great-aunt, Kate Woodcock, whose abiding and unconditional love inspired me in years jointly shared.

ACKNOWLEDGEMENTS

Before and during the work toward the publishing of this book, my family has been a stalwart unit of support, encouragement and love. In addition to my daughters, to whom this book is dedicated, my heartfelt thanks goes to my sons-in-law, Daniel Wolfram and Corey Gavril; my grandchildren, Blane and Zane Northrop, Rain (Mrs. Hayden) Jensen and Justin and Hannah Wolfram; and my newest joy, great-granddaughter Evelyn Reavey. I have received steady and constant encouragement from friends, especially MaryLou Shepherd, Lucia Sparks and Anne Vandergriff.

(THE OLD GRAY HOUSE)
WHERE THE DREAMS DIED

Tire swing
Kiddie things
Strawberry patch

Playing school
"April Fool!"
Pitch and catch

Summer ice cream
Happy wife dreams
Truth unfolding

His affairs
Her despair
Dreams die slowly

Tranquil farm
Lost its charm
How she cried…

…And went away
From the house of gray
Where the dreams died

TIME'S BLENDING

It's only a memory
In the Here and the Now,
That once-present Yesteryear
That slipped by somehow.

Dear things that I cherished,
Once real, once alive,
Have gone, died or perished,
And I see now that I've. . .

. . . Fought inevitabilities.
The Past's gone. It's GONE!
Relegated to memories
As Time marches on.

And on some bright Tomorrow
Time's balm will assuage
Today's hurts and sorrows
Til in memory's collage. . .

. . . Today blends with Yesterdays
And joy blends with sorrows
In diverse new ways,
Inviting Tomorrows.

DAY GOING DOWN

Late sun bright in the western sky
Illuming the day that is set to die,
To acquiesce to the evening soon,
To a navy heaven and a silver moon,

But not just yet, for the birds must play,
And the sun's last glow says, "It's STILL day!"
Nine noisy robins with burnt orange chests
Are bobbing for food on a spring green crest.

On a sapling limb quite close to the ground
A mockingbird flits and looks all around,
Paying no heed to this stranger at all,
Refusing to mimic my three-whistle call,

Choosing instead the buffoon to be,
An acrobat in a tiny tree.
Then even he, as if on cue,
Senses the day is nearly through.

In a matter of minutes the crest is bare,
And the gold/rosy glow is no longer there.
The buffoon has vanished in quiet flight,
And a cool breeze heralds, "Here comes the night."

With sleep, stars and darkness swift on their way,
You can see, feel and hear the last sigh of day.

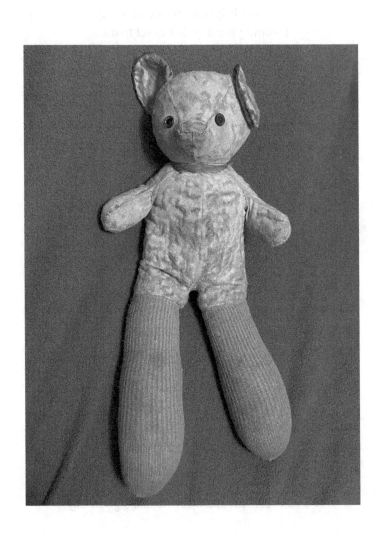

I PUT TEDDY AWAY TODAY, RACHEL

I put Teddy away today, Rachel. He's old and gray with grime.
His flat black nose and red felt tongue have disappeared with time.

His sparkling eyes are missing, and only the rims—
Round and black—remain intact. There's not much left of him.

Your daddy's light blue socks remain, that Grandma House sewed on
Teddy's feet up past his knees to catch the shredded foam.

Around his neck a ribbon pink she stitched with loving care
To hide a frayed but mended wound on cherished Teddy Bear.

I put Teddy away today, Rachel, action long overdue.
I know I should discard him, but I see in him so much of you . . .

The nights he slept beside you, the trips he made in your arms
From your birthplace in Reno, Nevada, to an Illinois farm.

And, oh, the things he's been to you! Your
teacher, your baby, your friend.
A thousand roles he played for you before the story's end.

You've worn his fuzzy coat threadbare, and who would ever know
That "once upon a time" his coat was soft and white as snow.

I've put him away before, you know, but he would never stay.
You'd miss him and you'd sobbing say, "Can me and Teddy play?"

And I'd give in, but that was then. Now things are not the same.
You're too engrossed in second grade to bring up Teddy's name.

Change must come if we're to grow, so on this very day
While you're at school with new-found friends, I've put your old one away.

I put Teddy away today . . .

Four little girls spanning four generations have worn the special heirloom dress. Top row from left: the author and her daughter, Jane. Bottom row from left: Jane's daughter, Rain, and Evelyn, daughter of Jane's son Blane.

JANE'S DRESS AND MINE

That sweet little flaxen-haired child, darling Jane,
Is skipping and singing her way up our lane.
Her smiling eyes rival the rays of the sun
In brilliance and warmth. Sweet Jane Allison.

She's skipping now closer as I catch a view
Of frolicky feet in shoes fresh and new.
Her dress—how old-fashioned! No, I've not forgotten
Those tiny white daisies on dark purple cotton

Cut from a flour sack and by Granny made
Especially for me in another decade.
When I was but five and toothless (in front)
I wore that same dress for a picture once.

I wore the dress often and liked it a lot
Until I outgrew it and almost forgot
It ever existed. Then one day 'while back
My mother came calling and held out a sack.

"I found this," she said, "in my old cedar chest."
Then opening the sack up, she held out a dress
Of tiny white daisies on dark purple cotton.
"You wore this to grade school. I bet you've forgotten,

"But I was just thinking that your daughter Jane
Might put this old dress into use once again."
It fits Jane quite well though a little bit long,
And watching her wear it brings memories back strong

Of worry-free childhood and worry-free days.
It's rejuvenating in so many ways.
The world and I both seem new, I confess,
When Jane skips and sings in that old cotton dress.

9

LITTLE MAN TWO

I think I love you, Little Man Two.
In fact, it's almost for certain,
You with the wasket in one of your baskets
And a jertain in your bedroom curtain,

You who've mastered the alphabet
And games on your parents' computer.
Four funny bunnies and three chicks are cute,
But Little Man Two's even cuter!

Could be that I love you, Little Man Two.
It's almost for sure that I do.
The words in your eyes and the hugs from your heart
Have made me addicted to you.

Perhaps I love you, Little Man Two;
I'll call when the answer is known.
Oh, I must quit writing now, Little Man Two,
For I'm being drawn to the phone!

I think I love you, Little Man Two.
This is no dream born of slumber.
Today is your birthday, Little Man Two,
And "Pointer" is dialing your number!

...

… Ring… Ring…

Blane, it's for you. It's Gramma.

LITTLE MAN THREE

I think I love you, Little Man Three.
I'm almost sure that I do.
Why would I otherwise feel so much glee
At the sight of--or the thought of-- YOU!

I think I love you, Little Man Three,
You with those little boy charms.
A very good place for you, Little Man Three
Is here in this grandmother's arms.

I'll squeeze and adore you, Little Man Three,
And listen to words you can read:
"God" and "good," "go," "cup" and "tree."
Very good! Yes, terrific indeed!

You're growing up fast, my Little Man Three,
As "quick as a birdie's blink."
I must decide if I love you...Let's see...
Yes, I love you for sure I think.

P.S. Can you guess the answer, my Little Man Three?

Just for the record: I love you.

- -

High
Low

I looked at the ceiling, and I got a feeling that the ceiling is higher.
I looked at the floor, then I thought some more, that the floor is lower.

THIS CHILD A LADY

In this child an old lady I see.
In my mind's eye she's quite elderly.
Her life's years I cannot foresee.
How wondrous I wish they could be.

Dear Lord, for a surety I know
She needs Thee and WILL need Thee so.
Please help her continue to grow
As through time and trials she'll go.

How serene, she lies here a sleeping.
Unforeseen, life's woes will come creeping.
Wash her clean in the storms that come sweeping.
May she lean on Thee, Lord, for safe keeping.

Her small hands now are folded in rest,
So sweetly, so soft, 'crossed her breast.
Oh please help her choose what is best.
And her days, may they be richly blest.

I pray this: that she'll ever thirst
For truth and put Thee ever first
And read and revere verse by verse
Sweet Scriptures that infidels curse.

You've nurtured your fold through the ages
As told in Your own sacred pages
And retold by each century's sages.
So please guide this child through all phases. . .

. . . Of life and when time comes to flee
Earth's shell may she find rest in Thee.
Neither child nor old lady, she'll be
Ageless in eternity.

THIS TIME I'LL TAKE THE OLD ROAD

I think I'll take the old road this time, not the new highway
That I've been traveling many a year. I'll take the old road today. . .
Through Kentucky and Indiana on my way to Tennessee.
What's different? What's the same as it was in the Used-to-be?

I wonder about the landmarks in the corners of my mind,
And even now before I start, I'm already hoping to find
Midway down twixt here and there that greasy spoon café
And a gaudy, aging jukebox with songs from then and today

Where for a single quarter six songs a gal could punch
And hum or cry whichever while waiting for her lunch.
I'll drive and scan the wayside for what's been gained or lost
And view the deep Green River we ferried oft across.

And that farm—do they still sell sorghum,
the kind that's a rich golden brown
And when mixed with creamery butter makes
a biscuit the best bread in town?
I'm aware of my destination, but there's joy in the journey, I've found,
So I'll survey the old haunts and places and
take one more long look around.

Yes, I think I'll take the old road. I wonder how it will be
To travel again as I did back then the old road to Tennessee.

The author's grandmother, Erma Woodcock, lived in Bugtussle
on the Kentucky/Tennessee border, so there was a Bugtussle
granny years before The Beverly Hillbillies television show.

GRANNY'S PLACE

Today I traveled down a road
I scarcely recognized.
It seemed to me the scenes of old
Were gone or in disguise.

So much has changed since I've been gone.
The woods by the road have been cleared.
People and sights that I had known
Have died or disappeared.

One house in particular caught my eye
And held it for quite a while.
Deserted…decadent…boarded up,
It brought, nonetheless, a smile

As I recalled a small lady –
Spectacled, aging, yet spry -
Who had flitted for years about that house
Like a bright butterfly in July.

It took my family half a day
To drive, years ago, to that place,
But all our weariness sped away
As soon as we spied Granny's face.

Out of the car we children flew.
"You all right, Granny," we'd say.
"I'm alive and kickin' I reckon, and you?
You all gettin' along okay?"

You could stand above Granny's old cellar
That opened out near the road
And look 'cross the woods toward Aunt Mary's
As evening began to unfold.

There whippoorwills called at set of sun
And on into the night
When Granny's coal oil "lame-ps" would burn
With flickering, shadowy light,

Faintly revealing her newspapered walls
And planks that comprised her clean floor,
Yet I don't ever once recall
Her bemoaning the fact she was poor.

Granny knew all the herbs in the woods
And how to use them, too.
She'd steep you up a tea so good
It'd make you feel like new.

While kindlin' crackled in the stove
She'd scurry around a spell
With fruit and flour and butter and love
And create a pie unexcelled.

She created paper flowers, too
And quilts in colors so bright
It cheered you to snuggle between them
And the old feather bed, come night.

But never lie with head facing east.
T'would be a terrible thing!
Why no telling how many months or years
Of bad luck such folly might bring.

And never rock a rocking chair
Unless someone is in it
'Cause if you do, then woe be you
Right from that very minute.

A thousand and one superstitions
Pervaded her simple domain.
If you should disregard that one or this one,
Shame! Shame! Shame!

She and her hoe killed copperhead snakes
And kept the garden weed free.
Her potted plants bloomed in and around
Her gray-siding house merrily.

Later she moved to a similar house
A mile or more away.
She's gone from there now, too, and forever,
Yet I can still hear her say,

"You all come back this way 'fore long.
I sure do wish you could stay."
Those yesteryears came back so strong
As I traveled her road today.

SILENCE IS SCREAMING FROM THE HILLSIDES

Silence is screaming from the hillsides
Where voices of loved ones once pealed.
It thunders from the bluffs and the hollow,
From the ridge and the untilled cornfield.

Silence, be quiet! For I hear now
My sweet mother's voice and guitar
And Dad talking business with Delbert
And Tucker's voice echoing far...

...Past the old echo shed near the garden.
His voice rings again and again,
Bouncing from the days of our childhood
And the shed even now as back then.

Now Silence is silent, for the voices
Are once again gone. All is still
As I stand alone here rememb'ring
My dear ones in graves on the hill.

HILLS OF MY CHILDHOOD

Hills of my childhood, I've come back to you
Seeking some solace for life gone askew,

Bringing my sorrows and tormented mind,
I come to you wounded yet hoping to find
Some comfort in memories, some balm in the flow
Of the branch and the creek—and the lightning bugs' glow.

Hills of my childhood, one of you folds
Earth hands 'round the caskets that tenderly hold
Dear ones that I loved—and lost--long ago.
(This current loss is far different though.)

I've spent some time at the Old Home Place
To gain enough strength the future to face.
Well, so long, sweet hills. I bid you goodbye.
You've helped heal a heart that was too hurt to cry.

Still here and still true, forever you stand,
My comfort when life doesn't go as I'd planned.
So hills of my childhood, when life goes askew
And I need some solace, I'll come back to you.

LURED IN

'Twas a fancy occasion I had dressed up to attend.
Now it's over, and I must be going.
My home county visit draws soon to an end.
Alone, I drive past tall corn growing.

"But wait! Don't leave!" I hear myself speak.
"Drive straight to the place you were born
And stop where the branch runs to merge with the creek
As it flows past the old family farm."

There, spanning the branch and the 39 years
Of the gulf between Then and Today
A young apparition on the far side appears
And joyfully calls out, "Let's play!"

That skinny blonde child is a part of the me
Standing grown by the branch today
With too-plump build and drab brown hair—
Well, the part that isn't gray.

The stifling summer sun beams down
'Til it's not even cool in the shade.
The forgotten yesterday's child resounds
In the mind of the lady, "Let's wade!"

Off go the dress shoes and in go the feet—
One bunion, two corns, hose and all.
Cool crystal ripples and tired ankles meet
As splashes and feet rise and fall.

Marching at first in an army of one,
'Til the child whispers sprightly, "Let's run!
Back and across and across and back.
Never mind rocks and gravel. What fun!"

Little girl, former self, you've made my day.
You've frolicked so carefree and sweetly,
And now as this lady from the branch turns away,
Say you won't EVER vanish completely.

ON A DAY LIKE TODAY
IN A YEAR LONG AGO

On a day like today in a year long ago
We romped o'er the farm, young faces aglow.
The sun was warm
And insects swarmed
On a day like today in a year long ago.

On a night like tonight in a year long ago
We chased after lightning bugs, charmed by their glow.
So young and carefree
My brother and me
On a night like tonight in a year long ago.

As I stand looking o'er a new farm yard today,
I'm a little bit plump and a little bit gray.
Two new little faces
Are taking the places
Of brother and me on that day.

I watch my two daughters, their faces aglow.
Joyful and lithe, they romp to and fro.
No longer carefree,
My mind's taking me
Wistfully back to that time long ago.

And I see that it's not the lightning bugs' glow
Or romping the span of the farm to and fro
Or youth, per se,
That I long for today.
It's the freedom from care I miss so.

CONTINUUM

The rains came.
The winds blew.
The rain froze.
The snow fell.
The sun came out.
And all was still . . . on Corinth Hill.

In a cabin at its base,
Grandma tilted back her chair
Against the porch at twilight time.
Grandpa played his fiddle fast.
Mother plucked a guitar tune.
Father could not play a thing –
Or sing—and so he listened.
I was young and Tucker new.
Aunt Kate was there, as always.

And the rains came.
And the winds blew.
And the rain froze.
And the snow fell.
And the sun came out.
Now Grandma rests on Corinth Hill.

Grandpa sawed a slower tune.
Mother sewed, and played guitar.
Father worked in a factory –hard.
I was growing and Tucker, too.
Aunt Kate was there, as always.

And the rains came.
And the winds blew.
And the rain froze.
And the snow fell.
And the sun came out.
Now Grandpa rests on Corinth Hill.

Mother worked in the PTA.
Father toiled on at the factory.
I played accordion.
Tucker played hooky.
We chased lightning bugs together.
Aunt Kate was there, as always.

And the rains came.
And the winds blew.
And the rain froze.
And the snow fell.
And the sun came out.
Now Father rests on Corinth Hill.

Mother worked in a discount store.
I took a mate.
Tucker took four.
Aunt Kate was there, as always.
Rachel was young, and Jane was new.

And the rains came.
And the winds blew.
And the rain froze.
And the snow fell.
And the sun came out.
Now Aunt Kate rests on Corinth Hill.

Mother fought leukemia,
I fought private battles.
Tucker fought in Vietnam.
Rachel was growing, and Jane was, too,

And the rains came.
And the winds blew.
And the rain froze.
And the snow fell.
And the sun came out.
Now Mother rests on Corinth Hill.

Tucker is losing the battle at home
Against his foe—the bottle.
I am in the PTA.
Rachel, in high school choir.
Jane's in grade school band—and sings.
Sisters, swiftly growing.

And the rains still come.
And the winds still blow.
And the rains still freeze
Beneath the snow.
And the sun beams down
On Corinth Hill...where all is still.

WRENS AND ROSES

She rode with me to Bible class
One day a week for a year.
The age gap existing between us
We did not let interfere

Or make communication hard.
She talked at a lively pace
With a merry twinkle in her eyes
And a sweet little smile on her face.

Though she was 50 years older than I,
She still had a keen, searching mind
And seldom mentioned how bad she felt
Or that she was fast going blind.

While many old folks choose to talk
Of the woes and pain age brings,
Emma chose instead to talk
Of lovely and lovable things

Like wrens and roses and mountains and spring,
The Bible and birds aloft in the sky.
"Little house wrens are the CUTEST things
And white roses make me cry.

"I like all flowers the good Lord made.
None should be underrated,
But the beautiful, delicate, perfect white rose
Is my favorite flower he created."

Emma lives now in the immortal realm,
Just one of the changes time brings.
Yet I think of Emma when I see wrens
And roses and lovable things.

STORM SONG

It looks as if the night is come too soon
As rain keeps pouring out of dim, gray skies.
The time is not as yet an hour past noon,
And though I cannot find him with my eyes,

He sings his cheerful presence in my ear—
That sweet song sparrow that I claim for mine
Though he is free as I—no, he is freer.
He glides from tree to tree to power line

On sunny days, and at the twilight time,
His clear sharp voice will surge to inspired height
In song that has no need of mortal rhyme,
In wordless song that sometimes charms the night.

And now here in this rain, this dismal gloom,
He sings unseen, though e'er so gladly heard,
In joyful notes that fill this dreary room
With hope transcending song of any bird.

Sweet song in stormy time can cheer our souls
While other broken spirits in the way
Take heart, as hope for them unfolds
In splendid glow beyond the present gray.

ONCE, COUNTING YOU

How many times have I given this ring to other lovers to wear?

How many times have I given this heart exclusively to share?

How many times have I risked despair by baring my soul in full view?

How many times have I told someone I cared enough to be true?

ONCE, COUNTING YOU.

MOTHER OF THE BRIDE

With a calm, steady stare
She watched him walk by,
Her tears long since dry,
But once how she cared.

There was no indication
She'd once been his wife;
He, her very existence, her life.
There was no indication

Of a bond once tight now totally undone.
Proudly he stands now
By their daughter who'll vow
Very soon to be one

On this white, floral day,
With the love of her lifetime
When her dad heeds the cue line,
When he gives her away.

Then the spotlight he'd shared
Turned back to the bride
And the groom at her side
While the bride who'd despaired

In the times gone before
Recalled, without tears,
Her own marriage years
As he passed by once more.

With a calm, steady stare
She watched him walk by,
Her tears long since dry,
But once how she cared.

A LIVE VALENTINE

What a happy Valentine Day it had been.
She'd been showered with gifts from family and friends—
Flowers and chocolates and cards, about ten,
And a bluebird of happiness gold lapel pin.

Beloved she was. Remembered, she'd been.
Happy she seemed, but empty within.
No, she'd not been forgotten. She knew people cared,
So why was that feeling of emptiness there?

Then the answer came swiftly, as if from above.
She missed the FEELING of being in love—
That wonderful, rapturous feeling of joy,
That life is for lovers, the whole world their toy.

She placed all her gifts on the TV stand
Then turned on the TV as she had planned,
Trying to forget it was Valentine Day
In hopes that the emptiness might go away,

But the very first scene that popped into view
Was lovers strolling two by two.
She cried to the walls of her lonely place
As tears streamed down her once pretty face,

"I want a LIVE valentine,
One who's exclusively mine for all time,
A live valentine I can count on to stay,
A sweet gentle heart that will not go away.

But not just ANY live lover will do.
He'll have to share my passions, too,
For music and art and literature,
Things that make life worth living for—

Rhymes that reveal deep thought of the soul,
Pictures that paint life as it unfolds,
Songs that lilt and lift spirits high.
Oh Lord, in this world is there still such a guy?"

Twice Dead

He sat on the bench in the heart of town,
Alone in a crowd, his eyes cast down,
Watching memories unfold on the ground,
Lost in the past as Today danced around.

Year after year, as time marched ahead,
He continued to live in a time now dead.
The phantom fire of a love grown cold
Burned on in the heart of a man growing old.

Though change followed change, HIS world stayed the same.
He still wore the ring, still whispered her name.
While people passed by on a fast-lane track
He'd wait for the past—and for HER to come back

For the day she returned would be the day when
The clock that had stopped would mark time again,
But the clock stayed stopped though a fire yet burned
In a gravely ill heart. Still, she never returned.

As life ebbed away, his friends felt bereft,
In truth, though, he'd died on the day that she left
Except for the mem'ries that had danced in the head
--For 23 years—of a man now twice dead.

AN OLD COUNTRY ROCKER

It was just an old country rocker, but, my, it was so wide and tall!
I remembered it well, or so I thought, as my aunt and I walked up the hall

To an attic where it was stored, awaiting much needed repairs.
How long has it been since I've seen it? I
wondered as we climbed the stairs.

So long it had lounged by the fireplace of Great-grandfather's farm home.
And how many hours had I rocked away in that living room alone?

While grown-up folks did grown-up chores
and talked of grown-up things,
I rocked away to magic lands on magic chair arm wings.

It's many years now since Grandpa's been gone,
I thought as we topped the stairs,
But I still cherish the rustic charm and the memory of his rocking chair…

…The cane-bottom seat, the flat arm rests
with nail heads the size of a dime.
Yes, I remember that huge old chair regardless of passage of time.

Then casting my eyes across the room, I saw - not a **big** chair at all –
But rather an average size rocking chair, not wide in the least – or tall,

But the cane-bottom seat and the flat arm rests
with nail heads the size of a dime
Assured me indeed it was the same chair and
that we had both changed with time.

It had grown old and I had grown up. Now gazing anew I found
Where always before I'd looked **up** at it, today I stood looking **down**.

And sitting erect in the chair I felt the edge of the seat at my **knee,**
And I realized that way back when that's
about where my **ankle** would be.

"I remember it well, Aunt Roxie," I said, "and
thank you for saying it's mine.
Though old and frail, it means more to me than one new, fancy and fine."

Arising, I thought of years gone by. I turned and in mem'ry could see
A gentle old man in blue overalls, and grandchildren (brother and me).

Large-framed and tall, raw boned and gray,
Great-grandpa smiled from his chair.
Then I turned away to rejoin Today – and family and friends downstairs.

FAITHFUL FLOCKS

Flocks of geese
In long, strong "Vs"
Forged on through the air
In days gone by,
Yet they still fly,
Fewer today but still there.

Now a human flock
Is scorned and mocked
'Cause they wear the Good Shepherd's name.
He is shunned, denied,
Twice crucified,
Yet his flock, though few, strong remain.

I BELIEVE

A tiny baby in a virgin womb
Child Divine who became a man
With nail scar in each riven hand.
I never saw the empty tomb…

…But I believe.

Time and the elements have all but obliterated the
engraving on baby Selby Jay's gravestone.

TO THE BROTHER I NEVER KNEW

Little Brother I never knew,
Happy birthday to you.
Two short weeks outside the womb,
Fifty years in a tiny tomb.

Fifty years ago this morn
You, dear Shelby Jay, were born.
One year after you passed away,
I was born on a summer day.

Two years hence at the harvest time
Came a baby brother, yours and mine.
People would ask me always before
The size of my family, and I'd say "four".

Now as the only one left alive
I poignantly realize we numbered five.
Mother and Dad, now Jerrold, too,
Have left this realm to be with you.

You seldom crossed my mind until
I buried our brother up on the hill.

Little brother, how sad I am
Looking down at the little lamb
Engraved upon your tiny stone.
Baby Big Brother, I feel so alone.

But I have much work left to do,
So I'll go back and see it through,
Fully living each day I'm alive
Til once again we number five.

APRIL, HOW COULD YOU?

April, you've mostly been good to me.
You've rolled back the wintry gray.
You've given me sunshine, flowering tree
And graciously heralded in May.

April, you've mostly dealt kindly with me.
Your showers have been gentle and warm,
So why last year on your very last day
Did you send such a fierce thunderstorm?

And why, April, why on that dark, drenched day
In the wake of that pre-dawn morn,
Why did you take my dear mother away
When the whole earth was being reborn?

Or were you, sweet April, as helpless as I?
Was thunder and lightning and rain
A sign of your anguish, a wrenching goodbye,
A baleful outpouring of pain?

And what now, sweet April? With flowers of spring
You've come back, perennial friend,
But the dear soul you left with last year you can't bring
Back with you, oh never again.

This picture of Gladys Gass, the author's mother, was taken on September 24, 1982, her 64th (and last) birthday.

THINGS GRANDMA LEFT

We have Grandma's glasses.
We have Grandma's shoes.
We have Grandma's music,
And now we have the blues
Because we don't have Grandma anymore.

We have Grandma's pictures
Of captured by-gone years.
We have Grandma's favorite things,
And now we have fresh tears
Because we don't have Grandma anymore.

We have things she knitted,
Things that she crocheted,
Things that she embroidered,
And clothes of ours she made
E'en though we don't have Grandma anymore.

But we have Grandma's small, sweet smile
And cheerful voice which starts
To soothe and warm, as an afterglow,
Tugging at our hearts
Although we don't have Grandma anymore.

The clothes will age, the pictures fade,
And time will dry our tears,
But the joy and the love she left behind
Will radiate for years

In the lives she touched, in the friends she knew,
So we must go on as before,
Reflecting the good of a lady much missed.
We don't have Grandma anymore.

Through the Window I See

With Jane in her baby pink ruffles, drowsy and limp on my arm,
And Rachel so quiet beside me, alert to the oncoming storm,
We sat in the big city church house, its ceiling exalted so high,
And listened to heavy rain pounding the roof as it poured from the sky.

But listen was all we could manage. We could not watch the rain fall
'Cause in that grand auditorium there are no windows at all.
Windows can be so distracting, some present-day planners maintain.
Yet binding our vision within stolid walls is much more a loss than a gain.

It breaks our link with nature and the pulse of the world outside
And the moods of the light and the darkness
and the elements all combined.
I'm glad my mind has a window—memory—through which I can see
Back to the days when I was the age of the child who's sitting by me,

Back to a church where along with the Word,
the sound of the hill country songbirds was heard,
Back to the days when flies could be seen
as they'd come a hummin' and light on the screen,

Back to a time when funeral home fans
would sway back and forth in work-weary hands
On hot summer days in the still, humid heat,
with sweat beads a drippin' on hard wooden seats.

It fills my heart with gladness to look out on the street
And see the big church buses coming in a fleet
To line up at the entrance and let the children file
Into the big church building with eagerness and smiles

To learn of God and Jesus and of the righteous way
That leads us on to heaven and strengthens us each day.
But in a tender corner of my heart I realize
That God does not judge churches exclusively by size

Or splendor of the buildings. That's not His way at all.
He seeks out those who do His will, whether grand or small.
God's great eyes can penetrate a window or a wall,
A low and humble meeting house or church with steeple tall.

Through bricks so thick or panes so thin, our Lord can see inside
And right on through to me and you – our
heart . . . our soul . . . our mind.

WHERE THE WOODS WERE

There was noise and loud commotion
When the county got the notion
To set "progress" in motion
On those thick green shaded acres
Where the woods were.

Flying squirrels sprang tree to tree.
Birds and beasties once lived free
Day by day and tranquilly
In those thick green shaded acres
Where the woods were.

But tycoons and concrete need space,
So Big Cats not only deface
But, worse yet, completely erase
Those thick green shaded acres
Where the woods were.

Poor Blind Seeing Girl

Poor blind seeing girl,
Look what you got yourself into.
See how you paid when you strayed
And craved what you knew was a sin to.

JAMES

Three feet high with bright blue eyes
And brown hair hiding his ears,
He shinned up trees, ran screaming from bees
But chased other bugs without fear.

He filled up his pockets with rocks and with sand
And with critters too precious to squash
Then stood at the table at mealtime with hands
So motley his Mom yelled, "Go wash!"

Seasons rolled past and the time came at last
(For James had become 82)
To gather the family to his bedside quite fast
To bid them one final adieu.

"We're all here, Dad, "his only son said.
"No, wait," said a daughter. "Where's Joe?
"That rambunctious boy!" said his mom in despair.
"I called him a short while ago."

"Here I am," said a boy with bushy brown hair,
Undaunted as he strode toward the bed
And smiled into eyes that resembled his own.
The child to his great-grandpa said,

"Pa James, here's the toad frog you asked me to bring
And these rocks I've been gath'rin'—and bugs."
The womenfolk gasp at the hopping small things,
But the boy was repaid with a tug

From the hand of an old man reliving the joy
Of childhood and youth, so beguiling.
Recalling the wonders of being a boy,
The old man then died—young and smiling.

The author's great-aunt,
Kate Woodcock. Her dour
countenance in photos
belied her warm and gentle
nature that endeared her
to nieces and nephews.

POSTHUMOUS LETTER
TO A FAVORITE GREAT-AUNT

Dear Aunt Kate,

You had a special way with kids,
A kind and easy way.
The funny things you said and did
Brightened childhood days.

You've been with me right from the start,
And since that Friday morn
That I was born at the Old Home Place
You've kept me in your heart.

When I was just a bit past two,
I moved with my parents away
To a factory town but we'd still drive down
To see you on Homecoming Day

And many holidays between
And vacation weeks as well.
The happy thoughts those visits brought
No words can aptly tell.

Walking along on a summer day
Up the path by the Old Home Place,
I pointed toward a flowering weed.
"Sister," you said, "that's white lace."

Later I learned when I grew up
The lace was officially "Queen Anne."
It still reminds me of you and that path
We walked along, holding hands.

You had no mate or child of your own
But nieces and nephews aplenty.
You loved them all, grown or small,
Infants and those way past twenty.

The year that I turned twenty-three
You met my "special friend."
Months went by, then he and I
Came to see you again

To tell you that we planned to wed
In the church at the top of the hill,
The first church I ever attended
And where we have homecomings still.

The rain fell hard in the old church yard
The night of my wedding day
And tears fell, too. I can still see you
Somber as I rode away.

You've waited at church each Homecoming Day.
You're waiting at church once again.
Today will be your last day there.
Today, Aunt Kate, is the end.

A song, a prayer, a eulogy,
And then they'll take you away,
Across the road to the graveyard.
I'll somberly leave and you'll stay.

Delaying the time of entering the church,
Delaying as long as I can,
I'll stop here awhile at the Old Home Place.
I know you'll understand.

Once family crowds, cheerful and loud,
Bustled around through these rooms.
Today like a shroud or an ominous cloud
The cold quiet veils me in gloom.

The wind—how it whips through windows and doors.
The glass is no longer there.
Things and people dwell here no more.
It's just a shell—stark and bare.

The March wind's howling through plants by the path.
It's too soon for white lace to bloom.
The sweet tiny bluebirds we used to watch
Are gone, too, and with them the tune

Of happier times and Homecoming days
In years that are forever past.
Our saddest "reunion" will be held today—
Our saddest, Aunt Kate, and our last.

But as long as I live, I'll see your face
At the churchhouse and on past the hill,
In every room of the Old Home Place
And out on that path by the rill.

I'll close with a "thank you" for memories
And for your abiding concern
That warmed me through years jointly shared
And helped me grow, love and learn.

Love always,
Carole

SHE CARED

She had no estate great to leave me,
No storehouse of wealth left to share.
Her treasure so free was a gold legacy—
It was just that she loved me. She cared.

In the eyes of the world she was nothing,
No outstanding talent, no flair,
Just a plain soul one safely could trust in.
Oh how she could stand by—and care.

She was quite ordinary in life and in looks,
Evoking no admiring stare.
She loved little children and small talk and books.
And when I needed a friend, she was there.

She left but a handful of things when she died—
Some clippings of poems and a prayer,
A faded old picture of friends by her side,
Young and smiling, near a school house somewhere. . .

Her mother's eyeglasses in a time-worn black case,
An old tablet that was falling apart,
Some tiny dried flowers in a small rosebud vase,
And a locket in the shape of a heart.

She left one thing that I didn't expect:
This feeling of loss I've since known.
She was SO low key that I didn't reflect
On her dearness until she was gone.

What a feeling of loss deeply planted!
I was somewhat surprised it was there.
I can see now how I took her for granted
Just because she loved me. She cared.

THE UNACCLAIMED

Here's to the aged and ill and alone
And those who seek to soothe them.
Here's to the myriad worthy unknown.
Some accolades are due them.

Here's to the many who fail to grasp fame
And those not inclined to the fray,
Who faithfully toil at a job mundane
Day after day after day.

Here's to the man of meager lot
Who condescends not to importune,
Who's thankful instead for the little he's got
And craves not another man's fortune.

Here's to the humble who hear no applause
And seldom receive any praise,
Who view with compassion other men's flaws
Though never condoning mean ways.

Here's to the faithful who hold the world up
On diligent shoulders, resigned
To do what is honest, avoid the corrupt
And yield not to greed, nor malign.

Here's to the sad who've suffered some loss,
And here's to the weeping ones
Who live with some handicap, carry some cross,
Yet bravely keep on keeping on.

When Christ comes again he may find some
Earth magnates hid—cowering. . .ashamed. . .
While the bulk of the ones redeemed will come
From the ranks of the unacclaimed.

Printed in the United States
by Baker & Taylor Publisher Services